S0-CYE-901

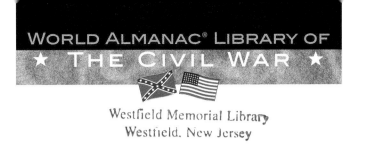

The Civil War in the East (1861–July 1863)

Dale Anderson

WORLD ALMANAC® LIBRARY

Please visit our web site at: www.worldalmanaclibrary.com
For a free color catalog describing World Almanac® Library's
list of high-quality books and multimedia programs,
call 1-800-848-2928 (USA) or 1-800-387-3178 (Canada).
World Almanac® Library's fax: (414) 332-3567.

Library of Congress Cataloging-in-Publication Data

Anderson, Dale, 1953-
    The Civil War in the East (1861-July 1863) / by Dale Anderson.
        p. cm. — (World Almanac Library of the Civil War)
    Includes bibliographical references and index.
    ISBN 0-8368-5582-5 (lib. bdg.)
    ISBN 0-8368-5591-4 (softcover)
    1. United States—History—Civil War, 1861-1865—Campaigns—
Juvenile literature. 2. East (U.S.)—History, Military—19th century—
Juvenile literature. 3. United States—Politics and government—1861-
1865—Juvenile literature. [1. East (U.S.)—History, Military—19th
century. 2. United States—History—Civil War, 1861-1865—
Campaigns.] I. Title. II. Series.
    E470.2.A53   2004
    973.7/3—dc22   2003062491

First published in 2004 by
World Almanac® Library
330 West Olive Street, Suite 100
Milwaukee, WI 53212 USA

Copyright © 2004 by World Almanac® Library.

Produced by Discovery Books
Project editor: Geoff Barker
Editor: Rebecca Hunter
Designer and page production: Laurie Shock, Shock Design, Inc.
Photo researcher: Rachel Tisdale
Consultant: Andrew Frank, Assistant Professor of History, Florida
    Atlantic University
Maps: Stefan Chabluk
World Almanac® editorial direction: Mark Sachner
World Almanac® art direction: Tammy Gruenewald

Photo credits: Library of Congress: title page, pp. 2, 12, 16, 18, 24;
Medford Historical Society Collection/Corbis: page 40; Peter Newark's
Pictures (American, Military and Western Americana): pp. 6, 7, 9, 11,
13, 14, 28, 29, 34, 36, 38; Corbis: pp 8, 10, 15, 21, 22, 35, 43; The
Granger Collection: page 27; Bettmann/Corbis: pp. 30, 32, 42.

Printed in the United States of America

1 2 3 4 5 6 7 8 9 08 07 06 05 04

Cover: Saving the Flag: A wheat field becomes a savage battle-
ground as Union Soldiers meet Rebel troops during the Battle
of Gettysburg in July 1863. Painting by Don Troiani, www.
historicalartprints.com.

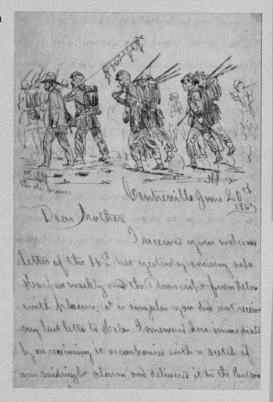

"To my mother, who got me
Bruce Catton; my brother,
who shared my passion for the
Civil War; and my wife and
sons, who cheerfully put up
with several field trips and
countless anecdotes."

— DALE ANDERSON

Contents

Capital cities
Union States
Confederate States
Seceded from Virginia
Border States
United States Territories

Confederate and Union States in 1861

While the Confederate states covered about as much territory as the Union states, they held fewer people, fewer factories, and fewer railroad tracks and locomotives. These would be significant drawbacks for the Confederacy during the Civil War. The South would also lose part of its support when West Virginia separated from the rest of Virginia in 1863.

The War between the States

The Civil War was fought between 1861 and 1865. It was the bloodiest conflict in United States history, with more soldiers killed and wounded than in any other war. It was also a pivotal event in U.S. history: It transformed the lives of millions of African-American men, women, and children by freeing them from slavery. It also transformed the nation, changing it from a loose confederation of states into a powerful country with a strong central government.

On one side were eleven southern states that had split from the United States to form a new country, the Confederate States of America, led by President Jefferson Davis. They took this step after Abraham Lincoln was elected president of the United

4

States in 1860. Southerners feared Lincoln would end slavery, which was central to their economy and society. The northern states, or the **Union**, declared this split illegal.

A big question was whether the four **Border States** (Delaware, Maryland, Kentucky, and Missouri) would join the **Confederacy**. They had slavery, too, but they also held many people loyal to the Union. To keep control of these states, Lincoln felt early in the war that he could not risk moving against slavery, fearing that to do so would drive the Border States out of the Union. Later, however, he did declare the **emancipation**, or freedom, of Southern slaves.

In the Border States, and in many others, families divided sharply, with some men fighting for one side and some for the other. The Civil War has been called a war of "brother against brother."

Fighting broke out on April 12, 1861, when gunners for the South began shelling Union soldiers in Fort Sumter in Charleston Harbor, South Carolina. This attack led Lincoln to call for troops to put down what he called an armed rebellion. Thousands of Northerners flocked to the Union army. Thousands of Southerners joined the Confederate army, determined to win independence for their side.

Soldiers in both the Union and Confederate armies suffered the hard-ships—and occasional boredom—of life in an army camp. They also fought in huge battles with great bravery and heroism. At times, both sides treated their enemies with honor and respect. At other times, they treated them with cruelty and brutality.

The opposing armies fought in two main areas, or theaters. The eastern theater included Pennsylvania, Virginia, and Maryland; the region near the Confederate capital of Richmond, Virginia; and the Union capital of Washington, D.C. The huge western theater stretched from eastern Kentucky and Tennessee down to the Gulf of Mexico and all the way to New Mexico. By the end of the many bloody battles across these lands, the Union won in 1865, and the states reunited into a single country.

Because it contained both capitals, the eastern theater was of vital importance to both sides. The Union began the war wanting to capture Richmond, hoping that to do so would end the war quickly. The Confederates, of course, had to prevent that. At the same time, Union leaders worried that the Confederates would mount their own attack on Washington, D.C. They made sure to always have troops near the city to prevent the South from taking it. These concerns shaped the planning of both sides in the first two years of the war.

CHAPTER ONE

A Bloody Picnic

~

The Confederate cavalry charges Union troops in the First Battle of Bull Run. The soldiers in the colorful red pants and fezzes were called Zouaves, named after French troops that served in North Africa.

Making "Armies"

In the spring of 1861, the North, commanded overall by General Winfield Scott, had amassed a force of 35,000 men near Washington, D.C. Approximately 20,000 Confederate soldiers led by P. G. T. Beauregard were camped just a few miles away at Manassas Junction in Virginia.

The recruits were hardly ready for battle, however. Both sides had difficulty getting food, weapons, and ammunition to their troops. Also, the volunteers had no military training. General Scott wanted time to train the new soldiers. But he feared that politicians would push for "instant and vigorous action, regardless . . . of the consequences." He was right.

In late May, the Confederates moved their capital from Montgomery, Alabama, to Richmond, Virginia. The presence of the "rebel" government just 100 miles away from Washington, D.C., worried many Northerners. As June dragged on, newspapers urged the army "on to Richmond."

There was another reason for Scott to attack. The volunteers in the Union army had signed up for just three months. In July, their enlistment terms would end. Northern leaders wanted to use the army before it went home.

General Irvin McDowell commanded the Union force near Washington. He developed a plan to attack the Confederates at Manassas. He did not, however, like the idea of an attack. He pleaded for more time to train the troops, who were "green," or inexperienced. President Lincoln did not want to waste time, and he told McDowell to march.

The First Battle

In mid-July, McDowell's army set out for Virginia. In the meantime, P. G. T. Beauregard received nearly 8,500 **reinforcements** at Manassas.

On July 21, McDowell attacked Beauregard's army. Many members of the U.S. government and Washington society came along for the show. They planned on enjoying a picnic lunch while watching the battle that would end the war.

McDowell's army attacked. Early in the day, it pushed the Confederates back. But Virginians led by Thomas "Stonewall" Jackson held firm. The fighting continued in the hot summer sun.

In mid-afternoon, Beauregard gained fresh troops and ordered his men to attack. The Union forces, who were tired from their marches and from fighting all day, began to fall back. The retreat quickly turned into a rout. Panicked soldiers dumped knapsacks and guns and ran back to Washington. "The further they ran, the more frightened they grew," one observer noted. Mixed in with the retreating soldiers were the equally scared Washington crowd, now fearful for their lives.

The battle—called First Bull Run in the North and First Manassas in the South—produced very few **casualties** compared to many later Civil War battles. The South's losses were about 400 dead and 1,600 wounded. The North suffered nearly 500 dead and over 1,000 wounded plus more than 1,200 missing or captured. Still, these numbers were much higher than expected. They were also higher than any battles in the Revolutionary War. The smoke and confusion of battle and the high numbers of dead and wounded left scars on both North and South.

But Southerners could console themselves with one thought. They had won the battle. Georgian Thomas R.R. Cobb wrote that Bull Run "has secured our independence." Northern newspaperman Horace Greeley—who had urged an attack—gloomily wrote Lincoln: "If it is best for the country . . . that we make peace with the rebels at once and on their own terms, do not shrink even from that."

CHAPTER TWO

"The Young Napoleon"

~

Union men spent the winter of 1861–1862 drilling and marching in formation in McClellan's effort to turn volunteers into soldiers.

Soldiers Wanted

First Bull Run made it clear to both sides that the hopes for a short, painless war were foolish. More troops were needed—and for more than just three months.

Before the battle, **Congress** issued a call for 500,000 volunteers to serve for three years. After Bull Run, a new law added another 500,000 Union volunteers, who were to serve for the duration of the war.

The South responded as well. The Confederate Congress passed a law allowing Southern president Jefferson Davis to recruit up to 400,000 men for three years. It also offered a $50 bonus to any of the original volunteers who reenlisted.

New Soldiers and New Commanders

Both sides also realized that they needed to prepare these volunteers for battle more thoroughly. In the east, the period from August 1861 to early 1862 was spent on training and getting arms and supplies.

The two presidents also named new commanders for their eastern armies. Jefferson Davis gave the command to Joseph E. Johnston, an experienced general. Union general McDowell had lost everyone's confidence at Bull Run. To replace him, Lincoln chose George McClellan, who had won two small battles in West Virginia. McClellan had a reputation as a brilliant military man. Many supporters called him "the Young Napoleon."

Some soldiers' families joined them in camp. Here, a Union soldier's wife earns money by doing soldiers' laundry.

Artists traveling with the armies created prints to illustrate magazine news stories on the war. This print shows the Union army on the march in Virginia in the spring of 1862.

"Little Mac"

McClellan turned tens of thousands of recruits into an army. He organized the force and imposed strong discipline. He also trained them well to move and fight together. Many soldiers loved him and fondly called him "Little Mac."

As the months wore on, though, he showed no signs of preparing an attack. McClellan said that Johnston outnumbered him, though the reverse was true. Some in the North wondered whether McClellan would ever attack. That concern grew stronger when Union troops entered a fort the Confederates had abandoned. They found that what McClellan had said were powerful cannons were nothing but logs painted black. People dubbed them "Quaker guns" because Quakers do not believe in fighting. Despite the discovery that the "cannons" could not fire, McClellan would not budge.

After McClellan became sick in December, 1861, it was clear there would be no winter attack from Union forces. A British journalist reported that all but one **diplomat** in Washington believed that "the Union is broken for ever, and the independence of the South virtually established."

Focusing on Richmond

By January 1862, Lincoln was losing patience. He ordered McClellan to move no later than February 22 that year. McClellan, having recovered from his illness, developed a complex plan that avoided attacking the Confederates at Manassas. Instead, he would move his army by ship to eastern Virginia and then make a short march to Richmond.

McClellan, like many others, thought that capturing Richmond would in fact end the war. The North assumed that the city represented a symbolic prize and that the Confederacy would not survive the loss of its capital. In truth, the South could have survived the fall of Richmond. The government could simply move to another spot. It took several years for Northern leaders to see that their real goal was to defeat the Confederate army, not simply to take its capital.

GEORGE B. MCCLELLAN

*George Brinton McClellan, born in 1826, graduated second in his **West Point** class. He had served well in the Mexican War of the 1840s. Later, he studied European fighting methods in the Crimean War, which Britain, France, and Turkey fought against Russia in the 1850s. When the war broke out, he rejoined the army.*

McClellan was a superb organizer. But as a field general he was slow to move and reluctant to fight. He also had a strong sense of his own greatness. "God had placed a great work in my hands," he wrote his wife.

McClellan constantly blamed others for his failures in battle. He bitterly complained about the army's top general, Winfield Scott, until Scott was forced to resign. He had a difficult relationship with Lincoln, once calling him "nothing more than a well-meaning baboon." His inability to be aggressive cost him his command.

After the war, McClellan returned to engineering. He also served as governor of New Jersey before his death in 1885.

On to Richmond!

~

A German-born officer named Ludwig Blenker
dedicated a song to George McClellan.

A Slow Advance

On March 17, 1862—nearly a month after President Lincoln's deadline—
McClellan finally began to move. He skillfully transferred a massive army and
all its equipment by boat to eastern Virginia. By early April, he had about
120,000 troops near Yorktown, Virginia. There he found a Confederate defensive line that stretched across most of the peninsula between the York and James
rivers. McClellan's advance was called the Peninsula Campaign.

Magruder's Bluff

The Confederate in command at Yorktown was General John B. Magruder. "Prince
John," as he was called, had only about 13,000 men facing McClellan's overwhelm-
ing force. To buy time for Johnston to come to the area, Magruder put on a show.

CHAPTER THREE

ALLAN PINKERTON

Feeding McClellan his information about the Confederate army was a man known in camp only as "Major Allan." His real name was Allan Pinkerton. Born in Scotland in 1819, Pinkerton came to the United States in 1842. The son of a police officer, he was interested in police work, though he was trained as a barrel maker. One day, he caught some crooks, an event which brought him into police work. Eventually he became a deputy sheriff. After a few years, he left the police to set up a private detective agency. His company investigated many railroad cases, which led him to meet George McClellan, then a railroad executive. After he took command of the Army of the Potomac, McClellan brought Pinkerton in to form an intelligence-gathering unit. Unfortunately, Pinkerton and his agents were better detectives than they were army spies. They dramatically overestimated the number of Confederates opposing McClellan. This misinformation simply fed McClellan's natural caution.

After the war, Pinkerton went back to his detective agency. His detectives were hired in several cases by companies trying to break up labor unions, and workers grew to hate "the Pinkertons." The detective died in Chicago in 1884.

A color print shows Robert E. Lee in a dress uniform. Though initially criticized in the South, Lee became idolized once he forced McClellan to pull back from Richmond.

heavy **artillery** so he could blast through the lines. Bringing the guns up took weeks. In the meantime, Johnston arrived at the scene. "No one but McClellan could have hesitated to attack," he observed.

But Johnston also thought that holding this line would be folly. One night in early May, he pulled his troops back. He set up a new defensive line north and east of Richmond. McClellan had lost another month.

Jackson in the Valley

Johnston had avoided a costly battle with McClellan's larger force. This preserved his much smaller army, but it annoyed President Jefferson Davis. Like Lincoln, he wanted to see his army in action. Robert E. Lee, Davis's military adviser, suggested a way to scare Washington. Lee's plan made use of Stonewall Jackson and the 17,000 troops that were in the Shenandoah Valley in western Virginia.

Starting on May 6, 1862, Jackson carried out a four-week **campaign** that is a model for using speed, surprise, and terrain to defeat an enemy. Jackson's force marched up and down the valley, attacking Union forces at will, and winning five battles—even though the combined Union armies outnumbered it two to one.

The campaign had its desired effect. It raised fears that Jackson

He had his men march around behind the lines, move cannons from place to place, and generally appear to be a much larger army than they really were.

McClellan took the bait. He stopped his advance, calling for would attack Washington. As a result, Lincoln refused to send McClellan the additional troops he had requested. Meanwhile, Jackson ended his Valley campaign and marched to join the Confederates defending Richmond.

The Gates of Richmond

By late May, McClellan's army was opposite Johnston's. Once more, he brought up heavy artillery. He planned to lay **siege** to the Confederate capital. At Davis's urging, Johnston attacked on May 31. The Battle of Seven Pines was inconclusive except for one thing. Johnston was wounded in the fight and was forced to give up his command. Davis named Robert E. Lee to take his place. Lee would prove to be a tough enemy for McClellan—and a string of other Union commanders.

A Dashing Ride

Robert E. Lee set his army to work strengthening their lines. They dug trenches and built wooden **breastworks** to hide behind. Southern critics, hoping for more action, called Lee "the king of spades."

Lee was willing to attack but wanted to know more about McClellan's army. On June 12, his 1,200-man cavalry force left on a fact-finding mission. Led by Jeb

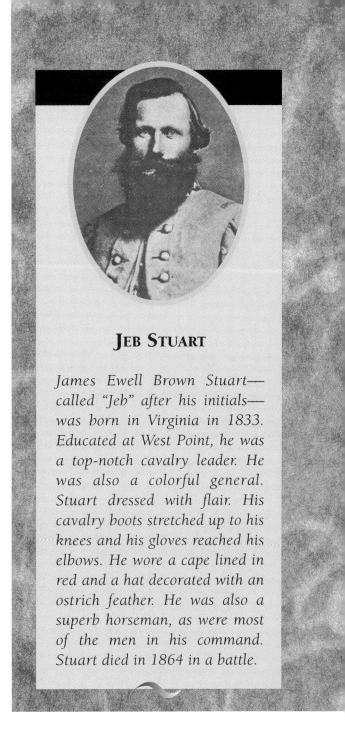

JEB STUART

James Ewell Brown Stuart—called "Jeb" after his initials—was born in Virginia in 1833. Educated at West Point, he was a top-notch cavalry leader. He was also a colorful general. Stuart dressed with flair. His cavalry boots stretched up to his knees and his gloves reached his elbows. He wore a cape lined in red and a hat decorated with an ostrich feather. He was also a superb horseman, as were most of the men in his command. Stuart died in 1864 in a battle.

Stuart, the Confederate cavalry got Lee the information he wanted. They also burned wagonloads of Union supplies and made themselves legendary by riding a circle around the entire Union army.

Joseph E. Johnston suffered a wound and lost the command of the Confederate Army at the Battle of Seven Pines. Note the Union's observation balloon in the sky on the left.

BATTLEFIELD TACTICS

Civil War generals patterned their **tactics** *on the victories of the French general Napoleon Bonaparte. Napoleon used one wing of his army to hold part of the enemy army in position. Meanwhile, another part of his force swung around to strike the enemy from the side, or* **flank**, *or from the rear. Such an attack prevented the enemy from bringing all its firepower to bear. Napoleon tried to ensure victory by attacking with more soldiers than the enemy had in defense.*

In Civil War battles, a full-scale attack in one area was often combined with a "demonstration" in another area. For instance, while Lee's left would attack McClellan's right, Lee would have his own right keep McClellan's left busy with a steady stream of fire. This would prevent McClellan from sending reinforcements from his left to his right.

These tactics were followed—by both sides—throughout the war. The plans often did not work, however. A major reason was the poor communication between parts of the army. Because of poor communication, the demonstration often did not take place at the same time as the main attack.

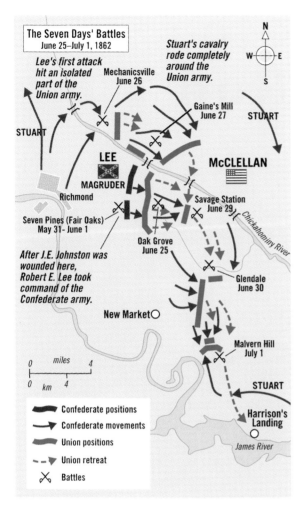

The Seven Days' Battles
June 25–July 1, 1862

Lee's first attack hit an isolated part of the Union army.

Mechanicsville
June 26

Stuart's cavalry rode completely around the Union army.

Gaine's Mill
June 27

STUART

STUART

LEE

McCLELLAN

MAGRUDER

Richmond

Savage Station
June 29

Chickahominy River

Seven Pines (Fair Oaks)
May 31- June 1

Oak Grove
June 25

After J.E. Johnston was wounded here, Robert E. Lee took command of the Confederate army.

Glendale
June 30

New Market

Malvern Hill
July 1

miles
0   4

km
0   4

STUART

Harrison's
Landing

James River

➤ Confederate positions
→ Confederate movements
➤ Union positions
- -➤ Union retreat
✕ Battles

The Confederates did not win a decisive victory in any of the Seven Days' Battles, but Lee gained his goal. McClellan pulled back from his threatening position near Richmond.

Attacks and Retreat

Stuart reported that McClellan had a lone army corps north of the Chickahominy River. The rest of the Union army was south of the river. Lee boldly massed two-thirds of his force against the isolated corps. John Magruder, in command of the 30,000 men in front of McClellan's main force, repeated his Yorktown tricks to hold McClellan in place.

On June 26, the Confederates attacked. They suffered heavy casualties and were unable to oust the Union force. The attack, however, rattled McClellan. The next day, Lee attacked again. This time the Confederates broke through the Union lines.

McClellan ordered a full retreat. Over the next few days, Lee attacked three more times as the Union army pulled back slowly. Each time his army suffered heavier casualties than McClellan's army. But McClellan continued to fall back.

Assessing the Battles

In the Seven Days' Battles—the fighting from June 25 to July 1—20,000 of the Confederate soldiers were killed, wounded, or captured, whereas the Union army lost almost 16,000 men. Though McClellan's army had won all but one battle, he felt beaten. He pulled his army back to a base on the James River, many miles from Richmond. Gloom spread throughout the North. "Things look disastrous," New York lawyer George Templeton Strong wrote.

Lee had forced a retreat by a larger army and ended the threat to the Confederate capital. No longer was he derided as the "the king of spades." Now Southerners called him a genius.

CHAPTER FOUR

Back to Bull Run

~

This print suggests that the Union soldiers drove the Confederates off at the Second Bull Run in August 1862. But it was the Northerners who once again retreated from the field.

New Leaders

McClellan's retreat lost him the confidence of his president. Abraham Lincoln brought in two generals who had won victories in the west. He named Henry Halleck as general-in-chief, charged with coordinating the work of all the armies in the field. Lincoln also placed John Pope in command of a large force in northern Virginia. Its job was to protect Washington, D.C., while McClellan was still in eastern Virginia.

Pope quickly outraged the men in his new army. He declared, "I come to you out of the West, where we have always seen the backs of our enemies." This implied, of course, that the Union troops in the east retreated. It won him few friends in the new army he led.

Lee Gambles

Lee was in a difficult situation. His 60,000 soldiers were badly outnumbered by McClellan's 100,000 men to his east and Pope's 50,000 to his north. He had to find a way to relieve the pressure on his army. Lee, a bold general, decided to attack. Logically, he decided to move against Pope, who had the smaller army. The only way he could defeat Pope's army, though, was to pull most of his troops away from Richmond and move them north. Otherwise, he would not have enough strength to take on Pope's army. Moving his army north would mean leaving only a small force between McClellan and Richmond. But Lee shrewdly decided that McClellan was too cautious to attack Richmond again.

Any idea that McClellan might have had of mounting a new attack on Richmond was eliminated by actions in Washington. Lincoln and others in the government feared that Lee would attack Pope and move on to threaten Washington, D.C. He

NAMING BATTLES

Many Civil War battles have more than one name. That is because the South called them by one name and the North by another. The Southern name often refers to the nearest town. The Northern name typically uses a nearby geographical feature. So the battles of July 1861 and August 1862 are called First Manassas and Second Manassas in the South after Manassas Junction. In the North, they are called First Bull Run and Second Bull Run after the creek that was an important feature of the battlefield. The September 1862 battle in Maryland was called Sharpsburg by the Confederates and Antietam, after another creek, by the Union. This series, like most histories of the Civil War, uses the Northern names.

ordered McClellan to take thousands of soldiers from his army and send them to strengthen Pope's force. McClellan protested, but the orders were carried out.

Taking his gamble, Lee moved against Pope. First he sent Jackson to attack Pope's supply base at Manassas. Jackson's men ate their fill of Union

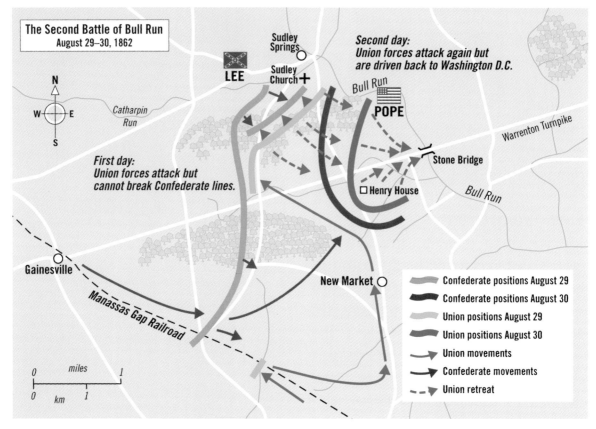

The Second Battle of Bull Run was fought over two days near Manassas, Virginia. This map shows a strong Union charge via New Market on the first day of fighting. When the battle ended, however, the smaller Confederate force had once again forced the Union army into a retreat.

Second Bull Run

On August 29, 1862, the Northern and Southern armies met once again near the Bull Run battlefield where they had fought a year earlier. Pope had about 63,000 men—including some from McClellan's army. Lee had about 54,000, though all of his army had not yet arrived on the scene.

Pope attacked first, but he sent his army against Jackson piecemeal, not taking advantage of his full strength. One reason was that Irvin McDowell—the loser at First Bull Run, who was now commanding part of Pope's army—was slow to move.

The Union soldiers could not break the Confederate lines on that first day. The next day Pope launched a fresh attack, but the Southerners once again held firm.

Then, in late afternoon, Lee launched a strong counterattack that pushed the Northern soldiers from the field. Once again, a Union army retreated from Manassas all the way back to Washington, D.C. It was a bitter defeat for the North. The Northern army had about 15,000 casualties compared to fewer than 9,500 for the South.

The Impact of the Battle

Though the Northern army had been beaten, the soldiers generally did not feel defeated. They had confidence in themselves—but not in their commanders. A Wisconsin soldier later recalled, "The feeling was strong in the army against Pope and McDowell. All knew and felt that as soldiers we had not had a fair chance."

The Southern victory added to the reputation of Lee and his army. In a few months' time, the Confederate commander had ended a threat to his own capital, forced two armies to retreat, and now threatened his enemy's capital. A Georgia lieutenant exulted: "Never in the annals of the world has a nation in such a short time achieved such history."

STONEWALL JACKSON

Lee's most reliable general was Thomas J. "Stonewall" Jackson. Born in Virginia in 1824, Jackson, like many other Civil War generals, attended West Point and served in the Mexican War (1846–1848). He resigned from the army in the early 1850s to teach at a military school.

Jackson was deeply religious, regretting a bad result in one battle that he waged on a Sunday. But he was a master of war. Jackson gained fame at First Bull Run, when he and his Virginia regiments stood firm on Henry House Hill. A colleague had tried to rally his own troops by saying "There is Jackson standing like a stone wall!" The nickname stuck, and Stonewall Jackson and his Stonewall Brigade became legendary.

Jackson moved his troops so quickly that they were called a "foot cavalry." When they arrived, they hit hard. From 1862 to 1863, Jackson and his men outmarched and outfought a string of Union opponents.

CHAPTER FIVE

Antietam: The Bloodiest Day

~

Horses pull cannons in the foreground while a long supply wagon is seen in the background. Moving the Union army required a huge effort.

McClellan Back

After the defeat at the Second Bull Run, Lincoln removed Pope and McDowell from command. He once more put all the Union troops in Virginia into McClellan's hands. He did it reluctantly—he had little confidence in McClellan. But he felt he had no choice. The decision was popular. One member of the army later recalled that "men threw their caps high into the air, and danced and frolicked like school-boys," when they heard the news.

Lee Invades the North

Meanwhile, the confident Lee had decided to invade the North. He had several goals. Doing so would allow his troops to feed off northern farms and give some relief to war-torn Virginia. Secondly, he hoped to find help from Southern supporters in Maryland. A slave state, it had many who sympathized with the South. Thirdly, he wanted to cut the rail line that ran east and west through Harrisburg, Pennsylvania. This would make it harder for western states to send food and soldiers to Washington, D.C. Finally, Lee hoped that a successful invasion would help the South diplomatically. Victories on Northern soil, he thought, might convince European countries to recognize the South's independence. Then they would give the South badly needed aid.

On September 3, 1862, Lee's army began moving north. Jefferson Davis ordered a simultaneous invasion in the west.

Lee Gambles Again

Lee wanted to keep a firm hold on the Shenandoah Valley so he could use it to bring up supplies from the South. That meant he had to eliminate a Union force at Harper's Ferry, at the north end of the valley. He sent Jackson to do the work and continued north with the rest of the army.

THE LEGEND OF BARBARA FRIETCHIE

Lee's invasion of Maryland resulted in a stirring—but not completely accurate—patriotic poem. In "Barbara Frietchie," John Greenleaf Whittier tells how the elderly Frietchie defiantly waved a U.S. flag from her house as Stonewall Jackson's men were marching through Frederick, Maryland. When some Confederate soldiers fired at the flag, Frietchie said, "Shoot if you must, this old gray head, But spare your country's flag." Jackson, moved by her courage, told his men to spare her.

Unfortunately, the incident never happened. Ninety-five-year-old Barbara Frietchie of Frederick did wave a U.S. flag at a marching army. But she waved it at Union troops, not Jackson's Confederates.

Once again, Lee boldly split his army in the face of a larger enemy. An aide wondered if this was a good idea. Lee responded that McClellan is "an able general but a very cautious one. . . . His army is in a very demoralized and chaotic condition, and will not be prepared for offensive operations—or

A photograph from September 1862 shows the small country town of Sharpsburg, Maryland, after the Battle of Antietam was fought nearby. Lee gathered his army here, though the position was dangerous. With the nearby Potomac River behind his troops, a serious defeat could trap his army if it was unable to get back across the river.

he will not think it so—for three or four weeks."

A Stroke of Luck

This time, Lee misread his opponent. McClellan moved more quickly than usual. He began to move his army to western Virginia and Maryland, trying to find Lee's forces. Then McClellan had an important piece of good luck. Near Frederick, Maryland, a Union corporal found three cigars that had a paper wrapped around them. The paper was a copy of the orders Robert E. Lee had given to his generals, which one of them had foolishly left behind. The orders detailed the position of all Lee's units on their march north.

McClellan was ecstatic. He told another officer, "Here is a paper with which, if I cannot whip Bobbie Lee, I will be willing to go home."

The Southern Position

Lee had good luck of his own. A pro-Southern Marylander had heard about McClellan's find and got word of it to

Lee. As a result, the Confederate commander was able to gather his scattered forces and take a defensive position before McClellan could hit him. His army grouped at Sharpsburg, a town in western Maryland. On September 16, Lee's army took positions north and east of the town. Lee's left held ground near some woods and a cornfield. The center was positioned on a sunken roadway. The right hid on high ground that overlooked a bridge across Antietam Creek. Lee had under 30,000 men on hand, with a few thousand more coming up from Harper's Ferry.

McClellan's Plan

McClellan had nearly twice as many troops—though he again believed himself outnumbered. He planned to launch a major attack on Lee's left. At the same time, another strong force would cross the bridge and hit Lee's right. This would prevent Lee from moving troops from there to his left. McClellan planned to overrun Lee's army wherever his forces broke through. He had four divisions of **reserves** in the center for that task.

For McClellan's plan to work, the attacks had to be coordinated. Lee had failed in the Seven Days' fighting because his officers could not coordinate their attacks. McClellan would have the same problem.

USING LAND AND WATER FOR DEFENSE

On his right at Antietam, Lee had soldiers stationed on high ground near the bridge over the creek. This made a strong defensive position. Usually, generals formed an attacking force in long rows hundreds of soldiers wide and several ranks deep. This enabled the attackers to hit a greater part of the defensive line. At Antietam, though, the Union forces attacking Lee's right had to cross a bridge to get over the creek. As a result, they had to move forward in columns just a few soldiers wide. Then they would have to form into attacking rows on the opposite shore. Meanwhile, the Confederate defenders had them as targets.

The defenders' job was made easier by being on high ground. This meant they could see—and shoot at—more of the ground in front of them. Throughout the Civil War, generals tried to place their troops on high ground to gain this advantage.

Woods, like those on the left of Lee's line, affected the battle also. Woods could hide troops, making it easier for them to move undetected. But they also made it more difficult for soldiers to march, slowing them down.

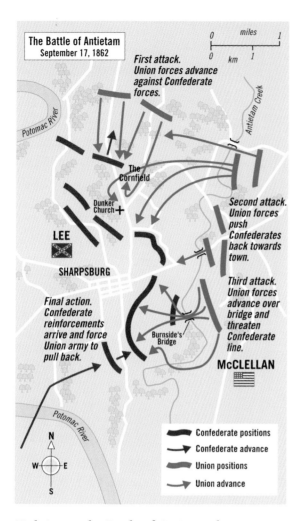

The Battle of Antietam
September 17, 1862

0   miles   1

0   km   1

First attack. Union forces advance against Confederate forces.

The Cornfield

Antietam Creek

Dunker Church

LEE

SHARPSBURG

Second attack. Union forces push Confederates back towards town.

Third attack. Union forces advance over bridge and threaten Confederate line.

Final action. Confederate reinforcements arrive and force Union army to pull back.

Burnside's Bridge

McCLELLAN

Potomac River

N
W—E
S

Confederate positions
Confederate advance
Union positions
Union advance

Fighting at the Battle of Antietam began north of the town of Sharpsburg early in the morning on September 17, 1862. It then moved to the center around midday and to the southern part of the battlefield—near a bridge over Antietam Creek—in the afternoon. A. P. Hill's Southern troops arrived from Harper's Ferry in the late afternoon, just in time to save the day for the Confederates. Still, Lee's army suffered a serious defeat and had to retreat the following day. This defeat decisively ended Lee's first invasion of the North.

The Battle

The Battle of Antietam, or Sharpsburg as it was known in the South, began as September 17 dawned. McClellan's troops came charging into the cornfield on Lee's left. The fighting quickly became desperate as Northern soldiers charged, Confederates counterattacked, and new Union troops charged again. Soon the ground was littered with bodies. McClellan had launched three corps in the attack, but they had come in waves, not all at once. That, as well as delays in the attack on the right, allowed Lee to move troops to plug gaps in his line. After five horrific hours, the fighting on Lee's left stopped. The two forces were exhausted.

Then the Union army struck Lee's center. The fighting was so fierce that the sunken road came to be called "Bloody Lane." The Northerners forced the Confederates to fall back closer to the town. If McClellan had launched his reserves into the fight, he might have destroyed Lee's army. But afraid of the additional troops Lee did not really have, McClellan held back his reserves.

By afternoon, the attack on the Confederate right finally began. When the Union forces finally won their way across the bridge, they threatened once again to collapse the Confederate line. Just then, Lee's last division reached the battlefield from

Late in the day at the Battle of Antietam, Union forces finally managed to stream across the stone bridge at the southern edge of the battlefield.

Harper's Ferry. Their counterattack forced the Union soldiers to retreat.

The Aftermath and the Cost

Lee stayed in position the next day to see if McClellan would attack again. The Union general did nothing. That night, Lee decided to take his army back to Virginia.

Antietam was the bloodiest day in the Civil War. In fact, it was the bloodiest single day in all of the United States's wars. More than 23,000 soldiers from the two armies were dead or wounded. A Pennsylvania soldier wrote, "No tongue can tell, no mind conceive, no pen portray the horrible sights I witnessed this morning."

Antietam was an important battle both militarily and politically. The Union victory there led the North to adopt a new goal for the war—the end of slavery.

CHAPTER SIX

A New Goal: Emancipation

The Political War in the North

While the Union and Confederate armies hammered each other in the field, Abraham Lincoln faced a tough political fight. **Abolitionists** were pushing him to end slavery. Frederick Douglass, a former slave and vigorous worker against slavery, demanded "the instant liberation of every slave in the rebel states." Newspaperman Horace Greeley published an editorial titled "The Prayer of Twenty Millions" in which he demanded that Lincoln act.

Lincoln resisted. He feared losing the support of Democrats. He feared losing the army—McClellan had declared that the army would not fight for emancipation. Most of all, he feared losing the Border States. If he ended slavery, these slave states might join the Confederacy. He also did not think that the president had the power to free slaves. The **Constitution**, after all, guaranteed people's right to own property, which, by law, slaves were.

Lincoln's final Emancipation Proclamation was issued on January 1, 1863.

Members of Lincoln's own party criticized him for this position. George Julian, governor of Indiana said: "When the history of this rebellion shall be written, its saddest pages will record the careful and studious tenderness of the administration toward American slavery."

The Issue of Contrabands

Meanwhile, African American slaves, through their own actions, were making themselves an issue. As Union armies advanced into the South, slaves escaped to them hoping to find freedom. Generals faced a dilemma. By law, the slaves were still property and should be returned to their owners. But commanders feared that the slaves could be used to help the Confederate armies by digging trenches, hauling goods, and raising food. Also, some Union generals were bitterly opposed to slavery. One of those was Union General Ben Butler, who came up with a clever solution to the problem. In 1861, he declared three such escaped slaves as "contrabands of war." That is, they were property seized from an enemy, just like wagons, animals, or food. Escaped slaves were called "contrabands" for the rest of the war. Over time, thousands of "contrabands" joined Union armies.

HORACE GREELEY

Horace Greeley was a determined reformer. Born in 1811 in New Hampshire, he came to New York City in the 1830s to edit a magazine. In 1841, he founded a newspaper, the New York Tribune. In its editorials, he pushed for many reforms. A strong abolitionist, he became an important figure in the Republican party. From the start of the war, he urged Lincoln to make ending slavery one of the goals of the Civil War. After the war, he continued to push reform causes. In 1872, he ran for president on a platform of ending political corruption. He died shortly after losing the election.

The Diplomatic War in Britain

There was another factor involved in the emancipation issue. Union defeats in 1862 had increased the possibility that the British and French would recognize Southern independence. If they started to give supplies to the South, the North would face a more difficult fight.

Some Northern leaders believed that by announcing the end of slavery, Lincoln could prevent Britain from supporting the South. In the early 1800s, Britain had declared the end of the slave trade, and the British navy had seized ships carrying slaves. These Northerners believed—correctly—that the French government would follow Britain's lead on the slavery issue because it would be unwilling to act alone.

Lincoln Decides

Early in 1862, Lincoln made some moves toward emancipation, though he did not yet adopt that policy. In March, he asked Congress to approve a plan that would free the slaves gradually, paying compensation to slaveowners. In April, he signed a bill that ended slavery in the District of Columbia. In June, he signed another bill that banned slavery from any U.S. territories.

This print makes neat and tidy what was actually painful and traumatic. The selling of enslaved people often meant the separation of husbands from wives and children from parents.

In August 1862, Lincoln answered Horace Greeley's plea to end
slavery. He explained that he saw the issue in terms of his main goal,
restoring the Union:

*"My paramount object in this struggle is to save the Union. . . . If
I could save the Union without freeing any slave, I would do it; and if
I could save it by freeing all the slaves, I would do it; and if I could save
it by freeing some and leaving others alone, I would also do that."*

He also made it clear that this did not reflect his personal feelings:

*"I have here stated my purpose according to my view of official
duty; and I intend no modification of my oft-expressed personal wish that all men everywhere could be free."*

Meanwhile, army commanders were coming to see the slavery question differently. Many at first had opposed ending slavery. As the war continued, though, they began to see freeing slaves as a weapon that could be used against the South. General Ulysses Grant summed up this view: "I am using [contrabands] as teamsters, hospital attendants, company cooks and so forth, thus saving soldiers to carry the musket. . . . It weakens the enemy to take them from them." Lincoln came to agree. At the same time, his idea of gradual emancipation was failing. Members of Congress from the Border States would not support the plan, as he had hoped they would. The President realized that gradual emancipation would not work—it would be all or nothing.

By July 1862, Lincoln had decided that he would indeed free the slaves. When he told his **cabinet**, Secretary of State William Seward suggested he wait. Since McClellan had just pulled back from Richmond, he said, it might seem that the decision was an act of desperation. Wait until the North wins an important victory, he suggested. Lincoln agreed.

The Emancipation Proclamation

Antietam, September 1862, was the victory Lincoln was waiting for.

On September 22, 1862, President Lincoln *(third from left)* read his draft of the Emancipation Proclamation to his cabinet. Secretary of State William Seward, who urged him to wait for a Northern victory before issuing the Proclamation, is seated in front of the table.

Though McClellan had not crushed the enemy, he had ended Lee's invasion. On September 22, 1862, Lincoln issued an early version of the Emancipation Proclamation. In it, he stated that unless the rebellion ended, all slaves in the rebelling states would become free.

On January 1, 1863, Lincoln issued the final Emancipation Proclamation. It stated that all slaves within the South "are, and henceforward shall be free." Lincoln went further than he had the previous September, then he also stated that the Union would accept blacks as soldiers.

The Diplomatic Result

Lincoln's proclamation came at a good time. On September 14, 1862, British Prime Minister Lord Palmerston had written to his foreign minister that "Washington and Baltimore may fall into the hands of the Confederates." If so, he wondered, should Britain and France "address the contending parties and recommend an arrangement upon the basis of separation?"

In other words, Palmerston was thinking that Britain and France should put pressure on the North to accept a peace treaty that would grant independence to the South. In the view from Britain, then, the Union seemed to be on the verge of losing the war. President Lincoln would have an even harder time winning the war if Britain and France supported the Confederacy.

The Union victory at Antietam and the Emancipation Proclamation changed the picture. Lee's defeat made the future of the South less hopeful. And after Lincoln's proclamation, abolitionists in Britain rallied support for the Union. Charles Francis Adams, the U.S. ambassador to Britain, declared that the new policy "annihilate[d] all agitation for recognition."

THE EMANCIPATION PROCLAMATION

Lincoln's final Emancipation Proclamation might seem like a half-measure. After all, the document did not free all slaves. Those in the Border States, for instance, remained in slavery. So did slaves in parts of Virginia and Louisiana that were already under Union control. Why did Lincoln make these exceptions? Lincoln's proclamation based emancipation on "military necessity." He was freeing slaves to weaken the Confederacy. Since the slaves already in Union hands were outside Confederate control—and since he did not think a president had the power to make any change in their status—he did not free them.

Even though his action seems limited, it had several important effects. First, it did mean freedom for about 3 million people. Any blacks who escaped from the Confederate states to Union lines would enjoy that freedom. So would those who came under control of Union armies as those armies gained control over more of the South. Second, the action gave a new moral meaning to the war. In his Proclamation, Lincoln called emancipation "an act of justice." The North was no longer fighting only for Union. It was now fighting for both Union and freedom. This added goal ended all possibility that Britain and France would recognize the Confederacy and support it. The governments of those two countries were not willing to be seen as fighting for slavery.

*Early in 1865, Congress approved the Thirteenth Amendment to the Constitution, which ended slavery throughout the country. Late in 1865, the amendment was **ratified** by enough states to become official. That act is what really ended slavery in the United States, but Lincoln's Emancipation Proclamation was an important step toward that change.*

Lee Wins—
and Loses

~

Union engineers had to build bridges across the Rappahannock River
under heavy fire from Confederates inside Fredericksburg.

A Change in Leadership

After Antietam, McClellan dawdled rather than pursued Lee's army. Lincoln urged him to move, but it took him more than a month to get his army into Virginia. The exasperated Lincoln decided to remove McClellan from command. In his place, he put General Ambrose Burnside. Burnside modestly said that he "knew he was not fit for so big a command." He was right.

Fiasco at Fredericksburg

Burnside started well, moving his 110,000-man army quickly to Falmouth, Virginia, on the Rappahannock River. As did McClellan earlier in the year, he aimed his force at Richmond. He hoped to cross the river and move south to capture the capital before Lee could stop him.

The plan failed when **pontoon** bridges that his army needed to cross the river did not arrive for a week. Meanwhile, Lee's 80,000 soldiers arrived on the opposite shore. They set up a strong defensive line outside the city of Fredericksburg.

After the defeat at Fredericksburg, Ambrose Burnside lost the support of the generals in the army, many of whom openly spoke against him.

On December 13, 1862, Burnside hurled his soldiers at the well-placed Confederates. Lee's men simply fired away, mowing the attackers down. By day's end, Burnside's army had suffered nearly 13,000 casualties compared to fewer than 5,400 for Lee. An Ohioan reporter wrote, "It can hardly be in human nature for men to show more valor, or generals to manifest less judgment."

Lincoln Changes Generals Again

Lincoln realized that Burnside could not lead the army through another battle. He replaced him with Joseph Hooker—who called himself "Fighting Joe."

Hooker spent the winter refitting his army. This was a very necessary task. The army had fought several major battles during 1862 and had suffered thousands of casualties. It needed some time to rest, recuperate, and regroup. Hooker reorganized the army, which grew to about 130,000 soldiers as new recruits arrived. He also strengthened the cavalry so it could challenge Stuart. Meanwhile, he boasted of the great success he would have in battle.

The Road to Chancellorsville

In the spring of 1863, Hooker finally moved from Maryland into Virginia. Like Burnside, Hooker began well. In just a few days, he took 70,000 troops in a long circle to reach Chancellorsville,

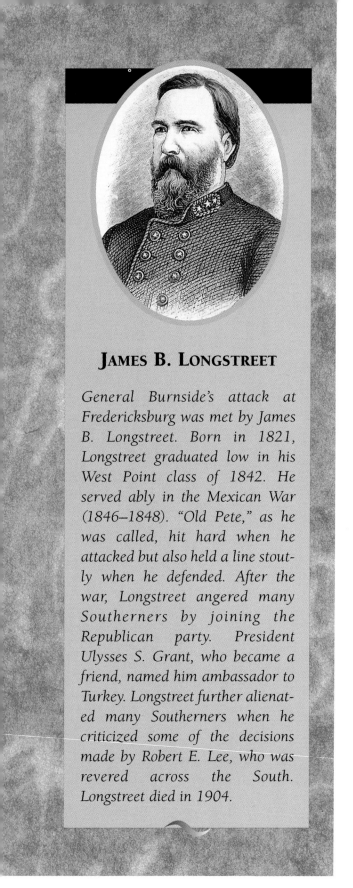

JAMES B. LONGSTREET

General Burnside's attack at Fredericksburg was met by James B. Longstreet. Born in 1821, Longstreet graduated low in his West Point class of 1842. He served ably in the Mexican War (1846–1848). "Old Pete," as he was called, hit hard when he attacked but also held a line stoutly when he defended. After the war, Longstreet angered many Southerners by joining the Republican party. President Ulysses S. Grant, who became a friend, named him ambassador to Turkey. Longstreet further alienated many Southerners when he criticized some of the decisions made by Robert E. Lee, who was revered across the South. Longstreet died in 1904.

a Virginia town north of Richmond. His other 60,000 men stayed in front of Lee near Fredericksburg. The Confederate army was now trapped between two large forces. Hooker announced to his soldiers that "the enemy must either ingloriously fly or come out from behind his defenses and give us battle upon our own ground, where certain destruction awaits him."

Lee's Surprise

But Lee was not going to permit Hooker to dictate the course of the battle. He left a small force of soldiers at Fredericksburg and moved the rest of his army toward Chancellorsville.

Hooker's army was in a good position, but one unit on the extreme right of the Union line was unprotected. If Lee could mount a strong flank attack on these soldiers, he felt he could overwhelm the Northerners. Once again, Lee split his army. He sent Jackson and the bulk of the force on a long march to the Union right.

In the late afternoon of May 2, 1863, Jackson attacked. The force of the assault threw the Union troops into a panic, breaking their lines. After a few hours of fighting, Hooker managed to patch a new defensive line together, and the day's fighting ended.

That night Jackson rode ahead to scout out the new Union positions. When he was returning to camp,

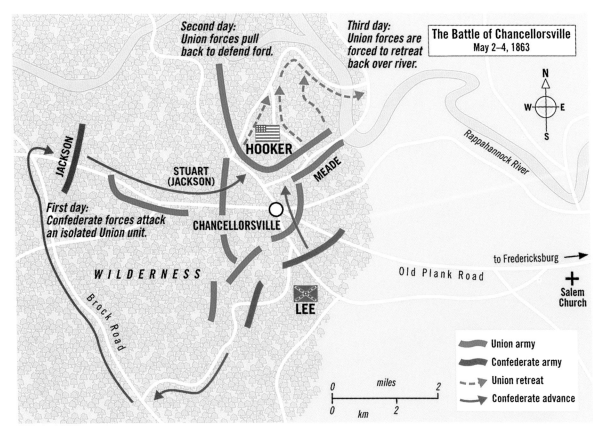

The Battle of Chancellorsville
May 2–4, 1863

Second day:
Union forces pull
back to defend ford.

Third day:
Union forces are
forced to retreat
back over river.

JACKSON

HOOKER

STUART
(JACKSON)

MEADE

First day:
Confederate forces attack
an isolated Union unit.

CHANCELLORSVILLE

WILDERNESS

Brock Road

LEE

Rappahannock River

to Fredericksburg →

Old Plank Road

Salem
Church

N
W E
S

Union army
Confederate army
Union retreat
Confederate advance

miles
0   2
0   2
km

While their main forces fought at Chancellorsville, other units of Hooker's and Lee's armies fought another battle to the east, near Fredericksburg.

Confederate guards mistook him for Union cavalry. They fired away, wounding Jackson.

A Costly Victory

Lee put Jeb Stuart in command of Jackson's part of the army. On May 3, he and Stuart launched a new attack. As the fighting became intense, Hooker was injured by debris falling from a building. He ordered the Union army to pull back to defend a ford that they could use to recross the Rappahannock River if needed.

The next day, Hooker's top generals urged him to counterattack, but "Fighting Joe" had lost his nerve. That night, he ordered the army back across the Rappahannock.

Chancellorsville was a brilliant victory for Lee. Hooker's army lost about 17,300 men compared to nearly 12,500 for Lee. It was a costly win, though. Lee lost his most trusted officer, Stonewall Jackson. After being wounded, he developed pneumonia and died. Jefferson Davis called his death "a great national calamity."

Gettysburg:
A Turning Point

This painting shows the climactic final attack on the third day of the
Battle of Gettysburg from behind Union lines. General Winfield Scott Hancock,
on horseback and pointing, directs the Union defenses.

Lee Moves North Again

After Chancellorsville, Lee's army was supremely confident. Time after time,
from early 1862 to May 1863, it had faced larger Northern forces in battle. Each
time, it had triumphed. The Confederates felt they could not be beaten. Once
again, Lee decided to invade the North.

His reasons were similar to those in 1862. He hoped to win British and
French aid for the Confederacy. He wanted to feed his army from Northern
farms and give some relief to Virginia. He also hoped that a Confederate victory on Northern soil would convince Northerners to push for peace.

Lincoln Changes Command Again

While Lee marched north, Hooker sat still. When he finally did move, it was slowly. This behavior exasperated Lincoln. He fired Hooker and replaced him with General George Gordon Meade. In just three days, the new, untested commander would have to lead his army in one of its toughest battles, which would be fought near the small town of Gettysburg, Pennsylvania.

Neither general planned to fight there, but the roads on which the armies were marching came together at that spot. Neither commander had a chance to scout the ground and decide where to position troops. Indeed, the troops arrived piecemeal

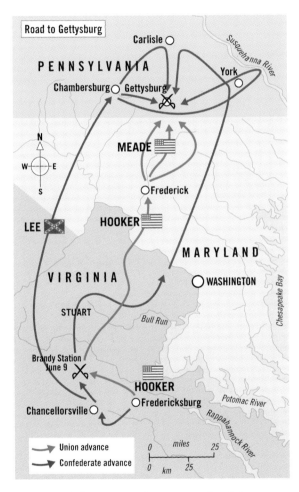

After his defeat at Brandy Station, Confederate cavalry commander Jeb Stuart wanted to regain glory. He tried to repeat his 1862 cavalry ride around the entire Union army. This ride, though, took longer than planned. As a result, Stuart could not scout the positions of the Northern army for Lee or help in the battle.

SHOULD LEE HAVE INVADED?

After Chancellorsville, General James Longstreet suggested that the Confederacy change its focus. Most of the army's attention had been put on the eastern theater of the war, the area around Richmond, Virginia, and Washington, D.C. He urged a shift of attention to the west, the large region west of the Appalachian Mountains. Longstreet argued that the South could save Vicksburg by sending part of Lee's army to eastern Tennessee to join Southern troops already there. This combined force could crush the Union army in that area and invade Ohio. That would force the North to pull away from Vicksburg to save the Midwest. Lee rejected the suggestion. He felt that the fighting in the east was more important.

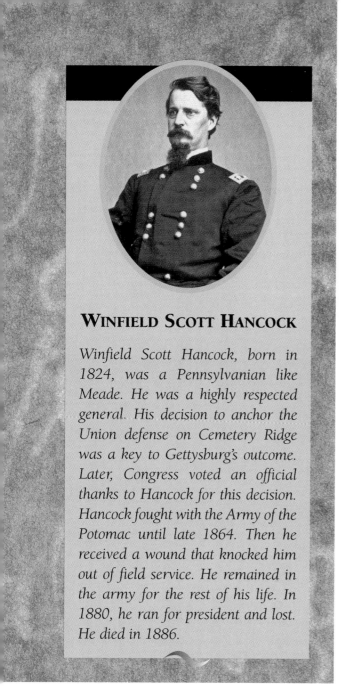

WINFIELD SCOTT HANCOCK

Winfield Scott Hancock, born in 1824, was a Pennsylvanian like Meade. He was a highly respected general. His decision to anchor the Union defense on Cemetery Ridge was a key to Gettysburg's outcome. Later, Congress voted an official thanks to Hancock for this decision. Hancock fought with the Army of the Potomac until late 1864. Then he received a wound that knocked him out of field service. He remained in the army for the rest of his life. In 1880, he ran for president and lost. He died in 1886.

Gettysburg. The battle began when a division of Confederates marched toward the town to find shoes rumored to be stored there. Instead of shoes, they met Union cavalry. The Northern troopers held off the Confederate attack for nearly two hours until Union infantry arrived.

As the day wore on, more troops from both armies reached the area. Each fresh regiment was thrown into the battle, and the fighting was fierce. A Confederate officer later said: "The two lines were pouring **volleys** into each other at a distance not greater than 20 paces."

Late in the day, a new Confederate onslaught forced Union troops to retreat to the southeast. They reached Cemetery Ridge, a long rise of high ground that stretched from the town of Gettysburg to the south. General Winfield Scott Hancock, a corps commander, decided that the ridge and two hills to its north would make a good defensive position. When Meade reached the battlefield that night, he approved. Lee, meanwhile, had his army west of Meade's and north of it.

The Second Day

On the second day, Lee hoped to dislodge the Union army. He ordered James Longstreet's men to attack the southern end of the Union line. At the same time, General Richard Ewell was

and had to be thrown into action as they showed up. It was an accidental battle but one that would have a profound effect on the rest of the war.

The First Day

On the first day, the armies fought north and west of the town of

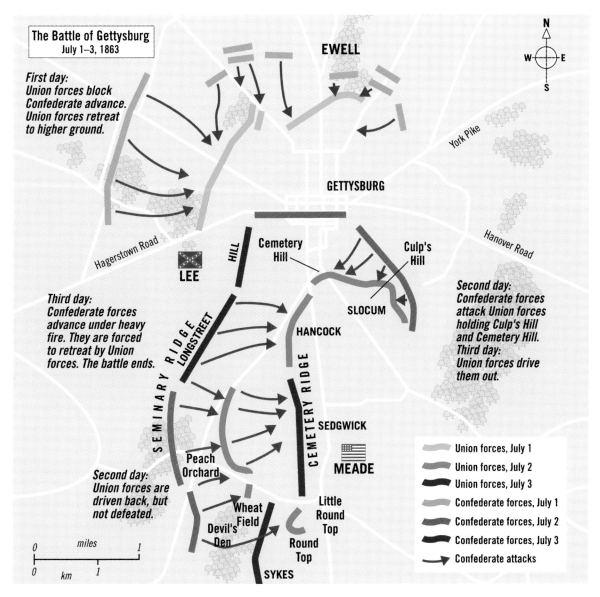

The Battle of Gettysburg
July 1–3, 1863

First day:
Union forces block Confederate advance. Union forces retreat to higher ground.

EWELL

York Pike

GETTYSBURG

Hanover Road

Hagerstown Road

LEE

HILL

Cemetery Hill

Culp's Hill

SLOCUM

Second day:
Confederate forces attack Union forces holding Culp's Hill and Cemetery Hill.
Third day:
Union forces drive them out.

Third day:
Confederate forces advance under heavy fire. They are forced to retreat by Union forces. The battle ends.

SEMINARY RIDGE

LONGSTREET

HANCOCK

CEMETERY RIDGE

SEDGWICK

MEADE

Peach Orchard

Second day:
Union forces are driven back, but not defeated.

Wheat Field

Devil's Den

Little Round Top

Round Top

SYKES

0   miles   1

0   km   1

Union forces, July 1
Union forces, July 2
Union forces, July 3
Confederate forces, July 1
Confederate forces, July 2
Confederate forces, July 3
Confederate attacks

On the second day of the Battle of Gettysburg, Union forces were on a line shaped like a fish hook from Culp's Hill and Cemetery Hill down Cemetery Ridge to the Round Tops. One part of the Union line, though, was farther west and isolated. A Confederate attack forced these troops back but could not take Cemetery Ridge.

supposed to attack the north end. By hitting both ends of the line simultaneously, Lee hoped to prevent Meade from reinforcing any weak point.

The plan failed, just as it had for McClellan at Antietam. Longstreet took many hours preparing his attack, which gave Meade time to strengthen his line. Ewell delayed his attack even later, allowing Meade to pull troops from his right to reinforce his left. Despite the heavy fighting—and near

Brigadier General Lewis Armistead, holding his hat on the tip of his sword, led his Confederate soldiers up to the Union lines during Pickett's Charge. Moments later, he was killed.

success by Longstreet's men—the second day of fighting ended with the two armies in more or less the same positions as before.

The Third Day

Lee decided to attack the Union center with 15,000 men under George Pickett. They would have to march across nearly a mile of open land and then overwhelm the defenders on Cemetery Ridge. General Longstreet protested, "I have been a soldier all my life. . . . It is my opinion that no 15,000 men ever arrayed for battle can take that position." Lee overruled him.

In the early afternoon of July 3, 1863, nearly 170 Confederate cannons began pounding away at the Union line to weaken the defenses. After a few hours, the cannons stopped, and Pickett's men set out. A Union soldier later wrote, "Beautiful, gloriously beautiful, did that vast array appear in the lovely little valley."

But Pickett's Charge did not have a chance. Union gunners blasted the Confederate lines. When the Southerners reached rifle range, the infantry just fired away. Some units

These three Confederates were captured at Gettysburg. Like many Southern soldiers, they did not wear regulation uniforms.

managed to reach the wall, but there were not enough soldiers to break through. Soon the remnants were retreating. "It's all my fault," Lee told his soldiers. "It is I who have lost this fight."

The Confederates began a long, sorrowful march home on July 4.

After the Battle

Both sides suffered horribly in the three-day fight. Lee lost 24,500 dead and wounded and another 6,500 missing or captured. Meade had nearly 18,000 dead and wounded and nearly 5,400 missing or captured.

The battle broke the power of Lee's army. The war would drag on for nearly two more years, but the South could never again hope to win the war by attacking. From here on, the Confederates were on the defensive. Their only hope was that the North would give up.

LINCOLN'S GETTYSBURG ADDRESS

After the battle, several Northern governors decided to create a cemetery to honor those who had died at Gettysburg. On November 19, 1863, a dedication ceremony was held. President Lincoln was invited to attend as an after-thought. Edward Everett, a famous orator of the time, was asked to give a major speech, which lasted two hours. Lincoln's speech—now called the Gettysburg Address—was much shorter. In it, he explained the meaning of the battle and also of the Civil War as a whole. He reminded lis-teners that the nation had been founded based on the idea that "all men are created equal." He said that the Civil War was being fought to ensure the survival of the nation and that idea. He closed by looking to the future:

"It is . . . for us to be here dedicated to the great task remaining before us—that from these honored dead we take increased devotion to that cause for which they gave the last full measure of devotion—that this nation, under God, shall have a new birth of freedom—and that government of the people, by the people, and for the people, shall not perish from the earth."

1860 *Nov. 6:* Lincoln wins presidential election on the strength of the votes from the North.
Dec. 20: South Carolina secedes.

1861 *Apr. 12:* Fort Sumter shelled, beginning the Civil War; surrenders on April 13.
July 21: Fierce fighting at First Bull Run (First Manassas) ends hopes of quick war.
July 22: McClellan given command of the Army of the Potomac.
Oct. 22: Johnston given command of all Confederate troops in Virginia.

1862 *Mar. 17:* McClellan begins to move his army by boat to eastern Virginia with goal of capturing Richmond.
Apr. 5: McClellan's advance on Richmond stopped at Yorktown; he begins siege.
May 3: Confederates evacuate defenses at Yorktown; McClellan has lost nearly a month.
May 6–June 5: Jackson's Confederates win several battles during Shenandoah Valley Campaign; many in Washington panicked by his success.
May 31–Jun. 1: Battle of Seven Pines (also called Fair Oaks); Johnston wounded; Lee placed in command of Army of Northern Virginia.
June 12–15: Stuart's ride around McClellan's army embarrasses North, thrills South.
June 25–July 1: Seven Days' Battles; McClellan pulls back from Richmond.
July 22: Lincoln informs his cabinet that he intends to free slaves.
Aug. 29–30: Battle of Second Bull Run (Second Manassas).
Sep. 3: Lee begins first invasion of North.
Sep. 13: Union soldiers find copy of Lee's orders revealing the positions of all units in his army.
Sep. 14: In fighting at South Mountain,

Confederates stop Union attacks.
Sep. 17: Battle of Antietam (Sharpsburg); McClellan ends Lee's invasion of the North but fails to destroy his army.
Sep. 22: Lincoln releases preliminary Emancipation Proclamation.
Nov. 7: Lincoln replaces McClellan with Burnside.
Dec. 13: Battle of Fredericksburg; humiliating Union defeat.

1863 *Jan. 1:* Lincoln issues formal Emancipation Proclamation, freeing slaves in Southern states.
Jan. 25: Lincoln replaces Burnside with Hooker.
Apr. 27: Hooker begins to move against Lee's army.
May 2–4: Battle of Chancellorsville; Jackson mortally wounded in Confederate victory, his loss weakens Lee's army.
May 30: Lee reorganizes his army into three corps to handle loss of Jackson.
June 3: Lee begins second invasion of North.
June 9: Stuart surprised in cavalry battle of Brandy Station; his angry response leads him to poor decisions before next battle.
June 28: Lincoln removes Hooker from command and puts Meade in his place.
July 1–3: Battle of Gettysburg; Union victory ends Lee's second invasion of the North.
July 4: Lee begins retreat back to Virginia.

1865 *Jan. 31:* House approves Thirteenth Amendment, abolishing slavery. The Senate had approved it in 1864.
Dec. 18: Two-thirds of the states having ratified it, the Thirteenth Amendment becomes official; slavery ended in the United States.

Glossary

abolitionist: a person who wanted to end, or abolish, slavery.

artillery: powerful weapons such as cannons and mortars that can fire highly explosive shells over a long distance.

Border States: the states of Delaware, Maryland, Kentucky, and Missouri, which had slavery but also had a large number of supporters of the Union.

breastworks: defenses made of wood that soldiers could hide behind to fire on an attacking force.

cabinet: a president's top advisors; the members of the cabinet are the heads of each department it includes.

campaign: a series of army movements aimed at achieving a particular objective.

casualties: the men killed, wounded, captured, and missing in a battle.

Confederacy: also called "the South;" another name for the Confederate States of America, the nation formed by the states that had seceded—Virginia, Tennessee, North Carolina, South Carolina, Georgia, Alabama, Mississippi, Louisiana, Texas, Arkansas, and Florida.

Congress: the branch of the U.S. government, made up of the Senate and the House of Representatives, that makes laws.

Constitution: the fundamental laws of the United States, which set up how the national government is formed, the powers of the three branches in that government, the relationship of the national and state governments, and the rights of citizens.

corps: an organizational unit in an army; in the Civil War, a corps included two to four divisions and had a strength of 20,000 to 30,000 men.

diplomat: a government official who handles a country's relations with other countries.

emancipation: the freeing of slaves.

flank: (verb) to attack an enemy force from the side; (noun) one side of an army in its field position.

pontoon: a flat-bottomed boat; many of these boats can be strung together and planks laid across them to make temporary bridges.

ratify: to formally approve an amendment to the Constitution.

reinforcements: soldiers added to a force to make it stronger.

reserves: troops initially held out of a battle so a commander can use them to add to an attack or reinforce defenders as needed.

secede: to formally withdraw from an organization.

siege: the bombardment of a fortified position with artillery, with the goal of forcing the enemy to withdraw or surrender.

tactics: the moves a commander makes to win a battle.

Union: also called "the North;" another name for the United States of America, which, after secession, included Maine, New Hampshire, Vermont, Massachusetts, Rhode Island, Connecticut, New York, New Jersey, Pennsylvania, Delaware, Maryland, Ohio, Michigan, Indiana, Illinois, Kentucky, Wisconsin, Minnesota, Iowa, Kansas, Missouri, Oregon, and California; in 1863, West Virginia seceded from Virginia and entered the Union as a separate state.

volley: coordinated firing of weapons by a large infantry force or a group of cannons.

West Point: the United States Military Academy, which is located in West Point, New York; West Point cadets were trained in science, mathematics, and military arts; upon graduation, they become officers in the army.

Further Resources

These resources cover the events and people of the first two years of the war in the east.

WEB SITES

www.civilwaralbum.com/ Civil War Album.com web site.

www.civil-war.net/ The Civil War Home Page web site.

www.nps.gov/anti/ Antietam National Battlefield web site.

www.nps.gov/gett/ Gettysburg National Military Park web site.

www.nps.gov/rich/ Richmond National Battlefield web site.

www.pbs.org/wgbh/amex/lincolns/ The Time of the Lincolns web site.

sunsite.utk.edu/civil-war/warweb.html The American Civil War web site.

BOOKS

Bolotin, Norman. *The Civil War A to Z : A Young Readers' Guide to over 100 People, Places, and Points of Importance.* New York: Dutton, 2002.

Cohn, Amy L., and Suzy Schmidt. *Abraham Lincoln.* New York: Scholastic, 2002.

Editors of Time-Life. *The Time-Life History of the Civil War.* New York: Barnes and Noble Books, 1995.

Grabowski, Patricia A. *Robert E. Lee: Confederate General.* Philadelphia: Chelsea House, 2001.

Index

Page numbers in *italics* indicate maps and diagrams.